The Scottie and The Squirrel

By Jeanne Bunting

Illustrated by Brigette Burns

ISBN-10: 1540735052
ISBN-13: 978-1540735058

DEDICATION

This book is dedicated to Addy, Kinley, Chloe, and Isaac.
Brodie is who he is because of you!

The Scottie Dog Adventures

ACKNOWLEDGMENTS

I would like to thank my daughter Skye for encouraging me and being my sounding board. I would also like to thank two of my friends who are also authors - Devan and L'Tanya for their enthusiasm and encouragement.

Thank you for letting me take a page from your book!

One day, a Scottie dog named Brodie, charged outside to play! Scotties are known to charge – ready to chase any critter they see, whether it's a lizard, a bird, a bug, or their favorite: a squirrel!

Sure enough, the squirrel Brodie had been chasing since he was a puppy was in the yard by a tree. Barking loudly, Brodie ran like the wind toward the squirrel, hoping to finally make a friend to play with. The squirrel, however, who had always mistaken Brodie's antics as a sign of danger, ran up the tree in fear for his life!

Brodie ran in circles around the tree trunk barking and jumping. In his Scottie mind he was asking the squirrel to play, but the squirrel mistook his barking as code for "that was close…he almost got me!"

Brodie got tired of running in circles so he ran over and pounced on a ball that his people roommate, Scott, had left lying in the yard. He bumped it with his nose a few times and then decided to throw it in the air to play catch with himself.

As soon as he bit into the ball, there was a loud POP!

Then, two things happened at the same time. First, Brodie dropped the ball, jumping back in shock. Second, there was a loud thump over by the tree. Well, that got Brodie's attention, so he sprinted over to investigate.

Lying on the ground was his 'friend' the squirrel...and he wasn't moving! Brodie gently nudged him with his nose but the squirrel still didn't move.

Brodie decided to lay down on his stomach with his head on his paws, watching for movement. Nothing.

Brodie got up and started trying to kiss his friend by licking him. Finally, after what seemed like forever, the squirrel twitched! Then, one eye popped open, then the other!

At first the squirrel was scared when he saw what he thought was his arch enemy bending over him. Then he realized that Brodie wasn't hurting him…

He was kissing him! When Brodie started licking his face the squirrel looked into his eyes and realized that, even though their bodies looked different, they were the same inside. They both just wanted to enjoy themselves and play!

From then on, on any given day, Brodie's people roommates would watch the Scottie and the Squirrel tumbling around and chasing each other in the yard. The very best of friends!

ABOUT THE AUTHOR

Jeanne is an avid Scottish Terrier fan and shares her home with one: Brodie! He is every bit as ornery and compassionate in real life as he is in *The Scottie and The Squirrel*! In addition to spending her time with Brodie, she enjoys her 5 grandchildren and resides in Topeka, Kansas. She has a master's degree in Liberal Arts with concentrations in Sociology, Religion, and Literature. Visit jeannebunting.com to stay up to date on Brodie and other titles!

ABOUT THE ILLUSTRATOR

Brigette Burns has been a working artist for 27 years and has worked in theater, puppetry, film, fine art, and photojournalism. She lives in Gallina, New Mexico and New York City with her french bulldog Gus. Learn more about Brigette and see her work online at- http://brigettemarieburns. weebly.com/.

ABOUT BRODIE THE SCOTTISH TERRIER

Brodie the Scottish Terrier is a loveable Scottie dog who enjoys playing in the yard and going on walks at the lake with his human. In his spare time one of his favorite things to do is to play with his little humans Addy, Kinley, Chloe, and Isaac.

Color Brodie the Scottish Terrier!

Color Brodie the Scottish Terrier!

Scottish Terrier Facts

1. The Scottie originated in Scotland. (Brodie's name is Scottish)
2. They are a type of terrier, meaning they were bred to burrow (Brodie loves to dig for critters)!
3. The Scottie dog is one of the most beloved game pieces in Monopoly.
4. Only two breeds have lived in the White House three times: the German Shepherd and the Scottie!
5. Most modern day Scotties can trace their lineage to one female named Splinter II. She is considered the mother of the breed.
6. They have won the Westminster Dog Show 8 times!!!
7. It takes awhile for Scotties to warm up to strangers – but not Brodie! He LOVES everyone!
8. They are very independent and self-assured. (Brodie is stubborn!!!)
9. Average weight for a Scottie is 19 – 22 pounds. (Brodie is a whopping 31! But not fat – he's just big for his breed).
10. They take praise really well, and they take blame hard (Brodie is very sensitive when he gets in trouble!)

More titles coming soon by this author!

The Scottie and The Bunny
Anthony and His Sister
Anthony and His Father
A Step In Time with History Rhymes

Made in the USA
Lexington, KY
01 November 2017